W A L L
dressing

Spectacular surfaces –
25 innovative applications

W A L L

dressing

Spectacular surfaces –
25 innovative applications

JUDY SMITH

PHOTOGRAPHY BY GRAHAM RAE

LORENZ BOOKS
LONDON • NEW YORK • SYDNEY • BATH

First published in 1997 by Lorenz Books

Lorenz Books is an imprint of
Anness Publishing Limited
Hermes House, 88-89 Blackfriars Road
London SE1 8HA

This edition distributed in Canada by
Raincoast Books Distribution Limited

ISBN 1 85967 224 8

A CIP record is available from the British Library.

Publisher: Joanna Lorenz
Senior Editor: Lindsay Porter
Photographer: Graham Rae
Stylist: Judy Smith
Designer: Caroline Reeves

Printed in Singapore by Star Standard Industries Pte. Ltd.
1 3 5 7 9 10 8 6 4 2

CONTENTS

INTRODUCTION

Wall decoration is probably the easiest and most immediate way of changing our homes. Whether moving house, or simply in need of a change, decorating walls allows us to express our personalities and moods, and make a real impact on our surroundings. The colours, patterns and textures chosen for a wall all dramatically influence the atmosphere of a room and are often the first things we notice when we go into somebody's home for the first time.

When we think about wall decoration, the first thing that comes to mind is usually paint. Indeed, paint comes in every colour imaginable, is relatively inexpensive, and nowadays is very easy to apply, so it is quite easy to overlook the wealth of other materials that can be used to enhance a painted wall. This book looks at new and innovative ways of decorating walls, without relying on specialist paint effects or home decorating skills. You may not feel confident about hanging wallpaper with a repeat pattern, but can apply simple paper cut-outs for decorative effects, devise your own stencils, or hang fabric, paper or filigree panels for visual interest. The projects in this book provide a rich source of ideas to help you make the most of colours, textures and patterns to create an impact in otherwise neutral areas. These can all be adapted to suit your space and your own tastes, so don't be afraid to use the practical instructions as starting points for your own ideas – once you start, you are certain to look at your walls in new ways.

USING COLOUR

Above: A strong burnt-orange colour will add warmth to a north-facing room, but will also benefit from the natural light of a south-facing room.

Nothing will single-handedly make such an enormous difference to a wall than the use of colour - and the bolder you are, the more dramatic the effect.

There are many things to consider when choosing a colour scheme, and the most important is, of course, your own colour preference. There is no point in following the latest design trends, or applying colour rules, if you are not happy with the final result. However, the following guidelines will help you reach a decision based on your own taste and style, and the requirements of the shape and size of your room.

Being bold with colour can be fun. Mixing brights together gives the most dramatic schemes, but as a basic rule, when mixing several colours, it is wise to keep to the same depth of tone. The tonal value of a colour is determined by the amount or white mixed into the pure hue – for example, pale pink is a tone of red. Another option might be to create a colour scheme based on tones of a single colour. You could, for example, explore the tonal range of a jade green by using it from its most pale and watery hues through mid-tones to its deepest colour. This will provide an interesting effect of layering colour that will be pleasing to the eye because it is based on a single colour.

Before choosing a colour scheme, you should take into account the aspect of your room. A north-facing room has cold light, a south-facing room warm, and this may make a difference to your choice of colour. You may want to add warmth to a north-facing room with colours such as yellow or burnt-orange, or you may want to make the most of the cool light, by using a Scandinavian palette of cool blues and pale shades. South-facing rooms can take most colours, particularly the bright, bold shades we associate with Mediterranean climates.

You should also bear in mind the proportions of your room, as colour will enable you to correct faults visually. Deep colours tend to bring walls inwards, and light colours give the illusion of pushing them away from you. A light colour will make a small area seem larger, while a deep colour will do the opposite. If

Above: The complementary shades of orange and blue create a dramatic impact.

Left: Blues provide a cool and calming effect in any interior.

you have, for example, a room with a high ceiling, you can create the effect of more harmonious proportions by dividing the walls in half horizontally, and painting the top half and the ceiling height in a darker colour. This will make the ceiling appear lower, which will be more in keeping with the small dimensions of the room. Following the same principle, a low ceiling can be made to appear higher by painting the top half of the walls in a light colour.

Whatever colours you decide upon in the shop, do take the time to look at your choice in the room itself, as the lighting conditions will be different. Look at the colours in artificial light as well, particularly if the room is used mainly at night. Remember that using colour should be fun; it's a great way of expressing your taste and style, and paint is relatively inexpensive, so you can ring the changes for a whole new look.

Above: A really strong colour can stand on its own, without added patterns.

BORDERS

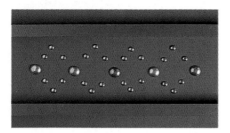

Above: A geometrical design of upholstery tacks makes an eye-catching border.

Below: Twisted ropes can be positioned at dado height to provide an unusual decorative feature.

Borders will give a room a face lift, and will add extra interest to a plain setting. The materials, colours, styles and patterns available are almost endless, so you can choose something individual, which also blends in with the style of the room. Borders can be design features in themselves, or be the finishing touch to a co-ordinated theme. You might choose an impressive frieze, a simple pencil line of colour or anything in between – all are impressive in their own way.

Add contrasting colour in a simple band of colour, or create a more complex design with unusual materials. Position borders just above the skirting, to dado- or picture-rail height, or even to where the wall meets the ceiling. Borders can run around windows and doors, be used to frame or emphasize a picture, or even make panels themselves.

You might consider using a stencil design for your border. There are many ready-made stencils on the market, from classical motifs to florals, and even nautical or seashore themes suitable for the bathroom. However, it is very easy to make your own stencil, and this will ensure the design is unique and totally yours. Simple chequerboards, diamonds and circles are obviously quite straightforward, but for numbers, letters or more complicated designs, it is a good idea to find the design of your choice, enlarge it if necessary on a photocopier, and then

Above: A simple chequerboard is easy to paint – simply mask out alternate squares and paint the desired colour.

Left: This quirky skirting-board is achieved deceptively quickly. The leopard-skin pattern is applied with a foam stamp.

photocopy the design on to acetate. Cut out the pieces with a scalpel or craft knife, and your stencil is ready to use.

Unusual materials also make fun borders and interesting edgings. Rope and string make wonderful curves, and can be fixed in wavy designs around the wall. Upholstery studs can be placed directly on the wall in a geometric design, and metal shapes, shells, pebbles or plaster decorations can all be fixed to the wall. With the help of a glue gun, you can attach just about anything. Simply work out your design on paper, mark out the wall with a spirit level to give you a rough guideline, and you're ready to start.

Wrapping paper can be cut and fixed decoupage-style along the wall, or you could cut out pieces of fabric to co-ordinate with other furnishings, or even stick newspaper headlines directly on to the wall. As long as you seal the pieces with a protective coat of varnish, almost anything goes.

Above: Two vibrant colours divide the walls in half visually, and are broken by and additional band of colour to create a border at dado height.

COLLECTIONS

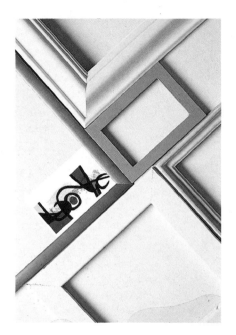

Above: Frames set on the diagonal create their own pattern across the wall. Hung on their own, they take on an abstract quality.

What could be more interesting and individual than a selection of objects that you have been collecting over the years? These make quite the most interesting additions to walls in any room of the house, and are absolutely individual to you.

Plates are an obvious choice because there are so many wonderful old and new ceramics available. Keeping to a colour theme gives cohesion to the collection, and makes it easy when you are out looking in junk shops or market stalls to enlarge your collection. These can be attached to the wall with wire holders, or you could fix strips of wood with a lip on to the wall, to stand the plates on. Small arrangements look pretty and add interest to nooks and crannies, whereas really large collections covering whole walls create real impact. As with all collections, placing them close together and confining them to a definite shape, such as a large rectangle or circle, helps the overall look.

Another fun idea is to group together small framed pictures. Again, keeping to a theme is fun, so you might want to frame and hang all your children's artwork, arrange a collection of black and white postcards, or hang a collection of maps. Using the same or similar frames helps the continuity.

Almost any collection of objects can be used as a wall treatment. Lanterns that can be lit at night would make a lovely addition to an entrance hall; baskets could be hung in rows in halls and kitchens to add warmth and texture to the walls, and have the added benefit of combining storage with decoration. You could also consider cups hung on hooks, collections of clocks, toys or almost anything – let you imagination run wild. The key is to keep the collection to a defined area for maximum impact.

Right: A collection of tin lanterns creates a delightful and eye-catching display. In a hallway they would provide a welcoming note.

TEXTURES

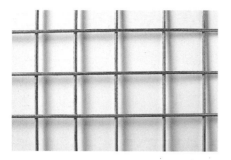

Above: A simple metal grille enlivens a plain wall.

Above: Rough plaster has its own particular charm.

Textures on the walls can open up a wonderful array of possibilties for new looks and styles. We often get no further than thinking of paint or wallpaper as wall choices, but there are many different materials that can be used to add extra warmth and interest, and make a welcome change around the home.

The most obvious choice is plaster – from an ordinary plastered wall that has been left its natural colour to a rough plaster effect that can give a Mediterranean feel. Kitchens and bathrooms look particularly good with rough plaster and, as these tend to be small rooms, it is less daunting to tackle a specialized effect. Plain white plaster looks wonderfully simple, but paint with translucent pastels or the deep ochres and terracottas of North Africa and you create a whole new style.

Wood is also very versatile. Tongue-and-groove can be added to the wall, up to dado height or beyond. By placing it horizontally, you can create an American East Coast feel. Paint it seaside-blue and white to carry out the theme, or experiment with different colours to change the effect. For a natural look, rub back the wood to give the effect of weathering.

Half-bricks may not sound the most fashionable of materials, but these don't have to be left in their natural state – they will look completely different with a coat of paint, and their style will change depending on the colours you choose. You could also consider inserting shells or pebbles into plaster. You can create a pretty mosaic effect, which is ideal for a small wall area such as a panel or splashback.

Sheet metal is now much more readily available than in the past, and again can look effective in the kitchen or bathroom, where there may already be lots of chrome and aluminium fittings and accessories. If you use it in a larger area, it is a good idea to keep it to panels or an area between the dado and picture rail so as to frame the metal.

It is also worth taking a look around builders' merchants to get other ideas.

Above: Horizontal tongue-and-groove evokes the seaside. The stamped motifs continue the theme.

Panels of filigree-effect board, usually used to conceal radiators, can be effectively placed directly on to a wall, and you can cut intricate designs out of them for borders and edgings. Plywood can be cut into shapes and then applied to the wall – anything from a jigsaw-type design to plain circles can be attached to the walls, and then varnished or painted. Corrugated plastic sheeting, trelliswork, strips of wood – all these different materials will add an extra dimension to the wall.

PATTERNS

Above: Colour is secondary to this lively combination of checks and diamonds.

The possibilities for patterns on walls are almost infinite – from the style to the size, the variations are endless. Of course, these include those patterns that are ready to use on wallpaper, but use your imagination to look beyond that to apply the pattern that is perfect for you.

Stripes are a simple option and, although there are lots of striped wall coverings available, it is incredibly simple to paint your own. Put on the base coat, mask out the stripes, and then fill them in with a toning or contrasting colour. You can be exact, and use masking tape to give precise lines, or try painting freehand for a looser and more carefree effect. You can vary the width from chunky to pencil-thin and use muted, toning colours, or brightly contrasting shades. Once you've mastered stripes, it is a small jump to checks, and again, these can take on any style, from the functional to the fantastic. If you are feeling bold, you can cover a whole wall, otherwise you might be content with the area beneath the dado rail, or in a smaller room such as a bathroom.

Circles, diamonds, zigzags or wavy lines, whether hand-painted or cut from coloured paper and pasted to the wall, make a bold and innovative decorating scheme. Be as adventurous as you like. By working out a pattern on paper,

Right: Sponge work is used for a pattern of controlled irregularity on this wooden wall.

Above: Paper circles in ice-cream colours were applied directly to the wall.

Left: Stamped designs strike a balance between the machine-like regularity of wallpaper and the spontaneity of freehand painting.

transferring it to scale on the wall, masking out sections and filling them in with colour, you'll be amazed at just how much you can achieve.

If you are looking for something prettier or more traditional, it's a good idea to look at the range of stencils and, more recently, stamps, on offer. Stamps work as the reverse as stencils, in that the colour is applied directly from the stamp on to the wall, which makes them very quick and easy to use. Use the pattern as an all-over motif, in panels, under the dado rail or along a border. The only problem you may find is, once you've started, it's difficult to know when to stop! Start off with some restraint, and keep looking at the effect before you continue. Remember, less can be more, and often the more selective you are with the pattern, the more effective the final result will be.

"ANTIQUE" MAP

Maps are both fascinating to study and extremely decorative, making them a wonderful wall treatment. Choose an up-to-date map for a child's room to maximize the learning potential. Elsewhere in the house, "antique" or old Ordnance Survey maps will look terrific. You can distress a new map to give it an aged appearance. You could even paper a whole wall in maps.

YOU WILL NEED

♦ tape measure
♦ pencil
♦ straight edge
♦ spirit level or plumb line
♦ map
♦ wallpaper paste
♦ pasting brush
♦ fine-grade sandpaper
♦ tinted varnish
♦ paintbrush

1 Measure and mark guidelines for positioning the map on the wall, using a straight edge and a spirit level or plumb line.

2 Paste the map to the wall as if it was wallpaper.

3 Distress the map here and there by lightly rubbing it with sandpaper.

4 Finish the ageing process by applying a coat of tinted varnish.

MOSAIC SPLASHBACK

Mosaics look complicated and elaborate but are actually very simple to do; you just need a lot of time and patience to complete the job. Use up broken tiles or look for chipped junk-shop finds to make a unique splashback for behind a wash basin. Stick to a simple colour theme, such as blue and white, or mix many different colours and patterns. You'll need a good selection of differently sized pieces to work with. Break up the tiles, plates and so on by putting them between two pieces of cardboard and hammering them gently but firmly; the cardboard prevents tiny chips from flying around. Working on a piece of MDF means that you can sit down with the mosaic on a table, which is less back-breaking than working directly on to a wall.

YOU WILL NEED

- ◆ tape measure
- ◆ MDF sheet
- ◆ pencil
- ◆ set square or ruler
- ◆ jig-saw
- ◆ drill, with wood and masonry bits
- ◆ beading
- ◆ mitre block and saw or mitre saw
- ◆ wood glue
- ◆ white emulsion paint
- ◆ paintbrush
- ◆ selection of broken tiles and ceramic fragments
- ◆ glue gun and glue sticks
- ◆ screws
- ◆ grout
- ◆ rawl plugs
- ◆ screwdriver

1 Measure the MDF to fit the width of your basin.

2 Draw your chosen splashback shape on to the MDF using a pencil and a set square or ruler.

3 Cut out the shape using a jig-saw.

4 Mark the position of the holes that will be used to attach the splashback to the wall. Drill the holes.

6 Glue the beading in place with wood glue, following the manufacturer's instructions.

8 Arrange the ceramic pieces on the splashback. Experiment until you have created a pleasing pattern.

5 Measure the beading that will frame the MDF. Mitre the beading with a mitre block or mitre saw.

7 When the glue is dry, paint the whole splashback white. Leave to dry.

9 Glue the ceramic pieces in place using the glue gun.

10 Put screws into the screw holes, to prevent you from grouting over the holes. Grout over the mosaic, being careful near any raised, pointed bits.

12 Glue on more ceramic pieces, to hide the screws.

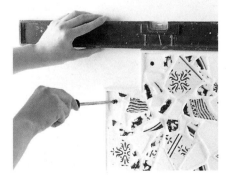

11 Drill holes into the wall and insert the rawl plugs. Then screw the splashback on to the wall.

13 Re-grout over these pieces.

A wonderful way to preserve favourite broken china fragments is to use the flattest pieces in a mosaic composition that makes a unique and durable splashback in a bathroom or guest room.

FLAG STENCILS

Here's a strong design to add colour and fun to a child's room, while avoiding the conventional motifs and colours available in ready-made children's wallpapers. The easiest way to make a unique stencil is to photocopy a simple motif on to acetate: here, two complementary flag motifs are combined. Use the stencils as a border at picture-rail or dado height, randomly around the room or in straight lines to make a feature of, for example, a chimney breast on one wall.

YOU WILL NEED
- ♦ acetate sheet
- ♦ craft knife
- ♦ self-healing cutting mat
- ♦ sticky tape
- ♦ black emulsion paint
- ♦ stencil brush or small paintbrush
- ♦ emulsion paint in several bright colours

1 Photocopy the designs from the back of the book at various sizes until you are happy with the size. Photocopy them directly on to the acetate.

2 Cut out the stencils carefully, using a craft knife and cutting mat. Tape the stencil to the wall.

3 Stencil a bold outline in black.

4 Use a stencil brush to apply colour inside the outline, or paint it freehand, for a looser, more childlike effect.

TRELLIS HANGING RACK

Ordinary garden trellis makes an effective hanging rack for any room in the house. Extend the trellis to make regular diamond shapes and then frame it with wood to give a finished look. You could confine this idea to a small area or join a few pieces of trellis together to run the whole length of the hall. Put hooks on as many crossovers as you want and collect decorative items to make part of the display, as well as the usual hats, umbrellas, and so on. Move everything about from time to time, so your display always offers something new to look at.

YOU WILL NEED
- ◆ tape measure
- ◆ pencil
- ◆ length of garden trellis
- ◆ hacksaw
- ◆ 2.5 x 2.5cm/1 x 1in wood lengths
- ◆ mitre block and saw or mitre saw
- ◆ dowel length
- ◆ wood screws
- ◆ screwdriver
- ◆ drill, with wood, metal and masonry bits
- ◆ burnt-orange emulsion paint
- ◆ paintbrush
- ◆ rawl plugs
- ◆ wood filler

1 Measure the area you want to cover and mark out the area on the trellis.

2 Cut the trellis to size with a hacksaw.

3 Measure and cut the lengths of wood to make the frame. Mitre the corners using a mitre block or mitre saw. Screw the frame together.

4 Mark the dowel into lengths and cut a notch in each length, to make hanging hooks.

6 Drill out any rivets where you intend to have hooks.

8 Paint the trellis and the frame.

5 Cut the dowel into lengths, using the mitre block or mitre saw.

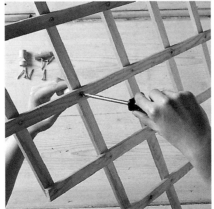

7 Position the dowel pegs on the trellis over the crossovers. Screw the pegs to the trellis.

9 Drill holes with a masonry bit and insert rawl plugs. Drill pilot holes in the trellis slightly smaller than the screws, to stop the wood from splitting, and then screw the trellis to the wall.

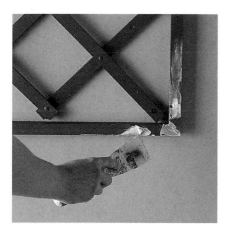

10 Fix the frame around the trellis by screwing it on to the wall. Fill and paint over the tops of the screws and any gaps. When dry, give the whole hanging rack a second coat of paint.

Right: Practical as well as eye-catching, this trellis rack can cover as large or as small an area as you wish.

WALL BLACKBOARD

This simple blackboard makes a practical and fun wall treatment for a child's room. Make sure the wall is flat before you start and give it an undercoat and two coats of emulsion, if necessary. Bear in mind the child's height when deciding on the size and position of the blackboard.

YOU WILL NEED

♦ tape measure
♦ pencil
♦ spirit level
♦ straight edge
♦ masking tape
♦ blackboard paint
♦ paintbrushes
♦ emulsion paint in several colours
♦ tracing paper (optional)
♦ craft knife (optional)
♦ self-healing cutting mat (optional)
♦ stencil brush
♦ hooks
♦ string
♦ chunky chalks

1 Measure and draw out the shape of the blackboard and the border on the wall, using the spirit level and straight edge. Mask off the basic blackboard shape with tape and paint inside the shape with blackboard paint. For a good finish, you will need two coats. Remove the masking tape immediately. Leave to dry.

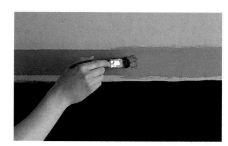

2 Mask off the border pattern. Paint inside the masked-off border with two coats of emulsion. Remove the masking tape immediately.

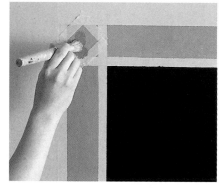

3 Mask off the diamond shape or draw and cut a stencil from tracing paper, using the craft knife and cutting mat. Tape it to the wall. Paint in the diamonds with a stencil brush.

4 Paint the hooks (you can even paint the strings to match). Screw the hooks into the wall and attach the strings and chalks.

BROWN PAPER PANELLING

Brown paper has its own characteristic colour and texture, which look wonderful on walls. You can buy it on rolls, which make papering under a dado rail simplicity itself. Here, the brown paper has been combined with gum arabic adhesive tape for an unusual and elegant interpretation of a classic interior look. You could also add a simple skirting-board, using 5 x 2.5cm/2 x 1in timber.

YOU WILL NEED

- ♦ brown paper
- ♦ wallpaper paste
- ♦ pasting brush
- ♦ plumb line
- ♦ pencil
- ♦ straight edge
- ♦ paintbrush
- ♦ gum arabic adhesive paper roll
- ♦ spirit level
- ♦ black beading
- ♦ glue gun and glue sticks

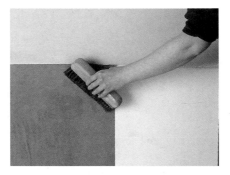

1 Stick the brown paper, matt-side inwards, to the wall, using wallpaper paste, as if it was wallpaper.

2 Use a plumb line and straight edge to mark vertical guidelines for the stripes on the brown paper. Using a paintbrush, wet the wall in a stripe the width of the gum arabic tape and stick the tape down. Make sure you cover up all the guidelines.

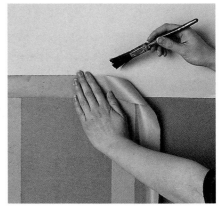

3 Use a spirit level and straight edge to draw a horizontal guideline for the under-dado border. Stick the tape in place in the same way.

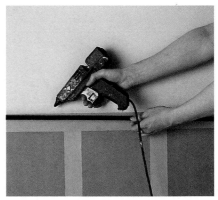

4 Attach the beading along the top of the border, using the glue gun.

TUSCAN DOORWAY

With patience and a little confidence, you can attempt a simple trompe-l'oeil *wall decoration, to create the feel of a Tuscan country house in your own home. The key to achieving this rustic look is to layer the colours and then rub the layers back to reveal some of the colours underneath, as though there has been a build-up of paint over years. The rest of the effect is created by masking off successive areas and finally adding simple freehand "coach lines", so called because they are similar to the decorative lines that embellished the liveries on horse-drawn coaches. In contrast to this traditionally immaculate finish, though, it doesn't matter if these lines become a bit wobbly: it just seems to add to the look! A final wash of watery ochre enhances the aged look.*

YOU WILL NEED

♦ emulsion paint in cream, yellow, terracotta and green
♦ paintbrushes in different sizes
♦ scrap paper
♦ paint roller
♦ paint-mixing tray
♦ pencil
♦ set square or ruler
♦ spirit level
♦ straight edge
♦ string
♦ masking tape
♦ hand-sander
♦ brown pencil

1 Experiment with colours. You can pick quite strong shades as they will soften when they are sanded back.

2 Apply the cream base coat.

3 Wash over this with a warm yellow.

4 Draw your design to scale on paper using a set square or ruler.

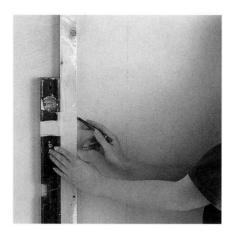

5 Measure and draw the straight lines on the wall, using the spirit level and straight edge.

7 Mask off the areas of terracotta colour with tape.

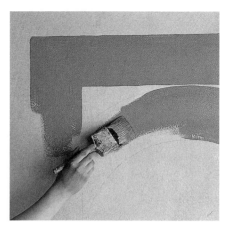

9 Paint the other areas green, masking off if necessary.

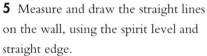

6 Draw the curve, using a pencil tied to a length of string.

8 Paint in the terracotta areas and immediately remove the tape.

10 Paint a thin yellow outline around all the edges by hand.

11 Lightly sand over the design, going back to the base coat in some areas and leaving others untouched.

12 Wash over everything again with the warm yellow.

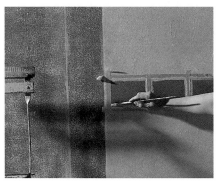

13 Mask off the squares in the border. Paint the outlines and immediately remove the tape.

14 Use the brown pencil to draw in extra fine lines in the semicircular "fan-light".

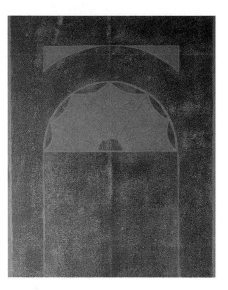

Above: The effective trompe l'oeil *design is simpler to achieve than it looks; its basic shape can be penciled in with the help of a piece of string used as a pair of compasses, and a ruler.*

Right: The look of frescoes, faded over the centuries by the hot Italian sun, can be re-created in your own home. The secret is to build up colour in layers and rub them back to different levels.

V I B R A N T   B L O C K S   O F   C O L O U R

For the boldest look of all, paint vibrant blocks of colour all over the walls. Using a basic square grid, work across and up and down to create strong patterns and changes of colour. Although this example is in very brightly coloured paints, you could choose a more subdued look, using complementary tones or much paler colours. Use this effect on all the walls in a room, if you're feeling brave, or confine it to one area, such as above a dado rail in a hall, for a less intense effect.

Y O U   W I L L   N E E D
- ♦ spirit level
- ♦ straight edge
- ♦ pencil
- ♦ scrap paper
- ♦ emulsion paint in several colours
- ♦ small and medium paintbrushes
- ♦ masking tape

1 Draw a basic grid of squares directly on to the wall using the spirit level and straight edge.

2 Decide on your colours. Putting small samples together on a sheet of paper may help you to decide which ones work together best.

3 Mask off the areas for the first colour. The blocks can be squares or oblongs, and they can turn corners, if you like.

4 Paint the blocks. Remove the tape immediately and leave to dry. Repeat the process for the subsequent colours.

SLATTED WOODEN NOTICEBOARD

This noticeboard makes a pleasant change from the utilitarian cork type. Using a darker shade of the same colour on the wooden strips gives the wall a co-ordinated look. The slats used here are 2.5 x 2.5cm/1 x 1in, but you could use a different size.

YOU WILL NEED

- ♦ tape measure
- ♦ wooden slats
- ♦ pencil
- ♦ saw
- ♦ smokey-blue emulsion paint
- ♦ paintbrush
- ♦ spirit level
- ♦ straight edge
- ♦ drill, with masonry and wood bits
- ♦ rawl plugs
- ♦ wood screws
- ♦ screwdriver
- ♦ tacks
- ♦ tack hammer
- ♦ bulldog clips

1 Measure the wood to the correct length and cut as many pieces as you will need.

2 Paint the wood in smokey-blue emulsion paint.

3 Measure and mark guidelines for attaching the slats on the wall using the spirit level and straight edge. Drill holes for attaching the wood to the wall and insert the rawl plugs. Drill holes in the slats and screw them to the wall.

4 Tap in tacks at regular intervals along the slats. Hang bulldog clips from the tacks.

PANELS WITH STAMPED MOTIFS

Bring large areas of decoration to a wall with these easy panels. Painting or dragging panels over a base coat quickly gives interest to large expanses of wall. It's a good idea to connect the panel and wall area outside visually with a simple motif. This could be a strong modern shape, wavy lines or even flowers. The colour of the walls and the style of the motif give scope for a wide range of different looks from the same basic treatment and, of course, you can vary the size of the panel to fit the shape and dimensions of the room.

YOU WILL NEED

♦ emulsion paint in cream, white and black
♦ paint roller
♦ paint-mixing tray
♦ spirit level
♦ straight edge
♦ pencil
♦ masking tape
♦ dragging brush
♦ scrap paper
♦ scissors
♦ high-density foam
♦ glue
♦ craft knife
♦ tape measure
♦ old plate
♦ small roller

2 Using the spirit level and straight edge, draw the panels on the wall.

3 Mask off the outer edge of the panels with tape.

1 Give the wall a base coat of cream emulsion paint.

4 Drag white emulsion paint over the base coat.

6 Stick the motif to the foam.

8 Decide on the spacing of the stamps and mark the positions on the wall.

5 Design the stamp motif on paper. Use cut-out shapes stuck to the wall to plan your finished design.

7 With the craft knife, cut out the unwanted areas of the design to leave a raised stamp. Angle the cut outwards slightly from top to bottom of the foam to give a cleaner finish to the stamped motifs.

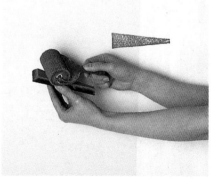

9 Put some black paint on to the plate, run the small roller through it until it is evenly coated and then roll the paint on to the stamp.

43

10 Stamp the design in the marked positions.

Right: The stamped motifs are clean and contemporary-looking, but more traditional or figurative designs can also be used.

PARCHMENT PAPER ART

There is such an interesting variety of textured and coloured papers available that it is easy to find the right basic ingredients to make some simple but extremely effective pictures, without being skilled at painting. Choose your colour combination and then make slits in the background paper, through which to weave the contrasting colours. These contrasting papers don't need to be clean-cut; tearing their edges actually enhances the finished look.

YOU WILL NEED

- parchment paper sheets
- coloured paper sheets
- scrap paper
- pencil
- metal ruler
- craft knife
- self-healing cutting mat
- drawing pins

1 Decide on the most interesting combination of papers. Use ordinary paper to plan your design.

2 Draw lines on the paper where you want the slits to be.

3 Cut these slits carefully, with the craft knife on the cutting mat.

4 Weave paper through the slits. When you are happy with the design, rework using parchment.

MATHEMATICAL MONTAGE

This is a fun idea for adding interest to a plain wall. The numbers and symbols have simply been enlarged on a photocopier. It doesn't matter if the black becomes streaked with white as the number is enlarged: this just enhances the hand-crafted look. It's best to keep to a fixed area, such as behind a desk, for maximum effect; just let the design fall away at the edges. You could also try musical notation behind a piano or letters in a child's room.

YOU WILL NEED
♦ craft knife
♦ self-healing cutting mat
♦ masking tape
♦ wallpaper paste
♦ pasting brush
♦ artist's paintbrush
♦ clear varnish
♦ varnish brush

1 Photocopy the numbers and symbols from the back of the book and enlarge them to various sizes.

2 Cut them out carefully with the craft knife on the cutting mat.

3 Try out the design first by attaching the shapes to the wall using small pieces of masking tape; move them around until you are satisfied. Or you can simply make a start and work out the design as you go. Paste the shapes on to the wall using wallpaper paste. Use the artist's brush to paste small and delicate shapes.

4 Give the whole design a coat of varnish, to protect it.

DECORATIVE CIRCLES

Wrapping paper and the papers used for walls and roofs of dolls' houses are now available in increasingly interesting designs and there's no reason why they can't be used on a wall. Confine them to a limited area, such as below a dado rail or within panelling, or use them more extensively all over the wall. Here, the wall has been painted a complementary colour to the paper and then circles have been cut out of the paper to reveal the colour behind; these circles are then used to make an interesting border.

YOU WILL NEED:

- ◆ scrap paper
- ◆ pencil
- ◆ coloured pencil
- ◆ wrapping or doll's house paper
- ◆ emulsion paint for the base colour
- ◆ paint roller
- ◆ paint-mixing tray
- ◆ round template
- ◆ craft knife
- ◆ self-healing cutting mat
- ◆ long metal ruler
- ◆ wallpaper paste
- ◆ pasting brush
- ◆ paintbrushes
- ◆ clear varnish
- ◆ varnish brush

2 Choose a paper with a small repeat pattern for the circles.

1 Plan and draw the whole design to scale on paper.

3 Choose your base paint colour to co-ordinate with the paper; it may help to paint swatches on paper to see how the colours work together.

4 Paint the wall in the base colour.

6 Decide on the spacing of the circles.

8 Cut out the circles.

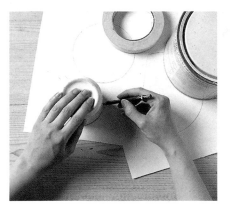

5 Decide on the size of the circles; you may have a plate, saucer or other round object of the right size, which you can use as a template.

7 Trim the paper, ready for pasting, using a craft knife on a cutting mat.

9 Paste the paper to the wall as if it was wallpaper. Be especially careful of the edges where you have cut out circles, as these are delicate. If you prefer, draw guidelines for positioning the cut-out circles; otherwise, position them by eye. Apply two coats of clear varnish, leaving to dry between coats.

Right: This idea would work just as well at picture-rail height as it does here at the height of the dado rail. The cut-out circles are graphic and the balance of the shapes is very pleasing.

BATTERIE DE CUISINE TILES

If you'd like to re-tile your kitchen but are short of cash, this is the cheapest imaginable way of achieving the effect: simple photocopies, pasted to the wall and varnished. Just find an appropriate motif that will fit neatly into a tile shape. After that, all you need is the patience to cut out and paste the copies on to the wall. You could adapt the idea to other areas of the house: just change the motif to fit.

YOU WILL NEED

♦ cutlery motifs
♦ pencil
♦ metal ruler
♦ craft knife
♦ self-healing cutting mat
♦ straight edge
♦ spirit level
♦ wallpaper paste
♦ pasting brush
♦ clear varnish
♦ varnish brush

1 Photocopy the motif as many times as necessary. Draw a tile-shaped outline around the photocopies.

2 Carefully cut the photocopies to the shape and size of a tile using the craft knife and cutting mat.

3 Using a straight edge and spirit level, draw guidelines for positioning the tiles on the wall to make sure you put the photocopies on straight. Paste the photocopies on to the wall, making sure you cover all the guidelines. Allow to dry.

4 Several coats of varnish will protect the wall and give a wipeable finish.

TA0884

HAND-PRINTED "TILES"

These imitation tiles are in fact paint, hand-printed on to the wall using a home-made foam stamp. This is a quick and cheap alternative to ceramic tiles and the potential colour combinations are endless: opt for tones of one colour, which is cheap, because you can buy one pot of paint and lighten it with white to get different tones; or use lots of contrasting colours. Making a stamp to apply the colour is a quick and foolproof way of getting squares of colour on to the wall. Don't worry about getting an even block of colour: slightly uneven colour gives an almost reflective quality, making the "tiles" look even more like the real thing. If you start with a white wall, the lines left between the fake tiles will look like grouting.

YOU WILL NEED

- ◆ ruler
- ◆ pencil
- ◆ scrap paper
- ◆ high-density foam
- ◆ glue
- ◆ craft knife
- ◆ self-healing cutting mat
- ◆ emulsion paint in 2 colours, plus white
- ◆ paintbrushes
- ◆ scissors
- ◆ straight edge
- ◆ spirit level
- ◆ old plates
- ◆ small roller
- ◆ small brush
- ◆ clear varnish
- ◆ varnish brush

2 Draw your design for the stamp on paper. Glue it to the foam and cut out the unwanted areas of foam with the craft knife. Angle the cut outwards slightly from top to bottom of the foam. It's best to make a separate stamp for each colour. For this design you will need six stamps.

3 Use a smaller piece of foam to make a handle on the back of the stamp.

1 Decide on the size of the tiles.

56

4 Choose your colours. Here, a scheme of six tones, made from two basic colours, was used. One-third of each colour was mixed together to make a third colour and then these three colours were halved again and one half of each lightened with white.

5 Decide on the repeat pattern; small-scale paper squares, painted in the different colours and/or tones, will help you plan the design.

6 Mark horizontal guidelines on the wall with faint pencil lines, using a straight edge and a spirit level

7 Mark vertical guidelines in the same way.

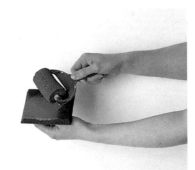

8 Put some paint on to a plate and run the roller through it until it is evenly coated, then roll the paint on to the stamp.

9 Stamp on to the wall, pressing down firmly with your fingers. Go around the "grout" area and touch up any smudges with white paint and a small brush. Make sure no pencil guidelines are visible.

10 Apply two coats of varnish to protect the surface and give it a wipeable finish.

Right: The stamped "tiles" are a witty addition to the bathroom, and are remarkably authentic.

PAINTED HALF-BRICK "TILES"

Thin brick tiles are widely available and can take on a whole new character when they are painted an interesting colour. You can arrange them in traditional brick-fashion, or one above the other for a different look. Herringbone and basketweave patterns are also possible. Consult a reference book of bricklaying patterns for ideas. As the right side is rough brick and the back is smooth, you can also have fun making patterns with the different textures. Halved and quartered bricks make interesting borders and more complex variations on whole-brick designs. The colour you paint the bricks is all-important; the same design painted white looks very different from ochre, for example.

YOU WILL NEED

- ◆ straight edge
- ◆ spirit level
- ◆ pencil
- ◆ thin bricks
- ◆ brick adhesive (check brick manufacturer's instructions)
- ◆ hacksaw
- ◆ pale yellow emulsion paint
- ◆ paintbrush
- ◆ grout (optional)

1 Use the straight edge and spirit level to draw guidelines for the positions of the bricks on the wall. Then, using adhesive and following the brick manufacturer's instructions, stick the bricks in place. Cut some bricks in half or in quarters with the hacksaw. Use the smaller pieces to make a border at dado-rail height.

2 Give the bricks a first coat of paint.

3 If you want, grout the bricks and then paint over the bricks and grout again. Otherwise, just give the bricks a second coat of paint.

GEOMETRIC WALL-BOARD

However unartistic you think you are, you can make a work of art for your wall and you can even make sure it's the right size and in complementary colours for your room! Taking a piece of MDF and keeping to a simple, repetitive design, you can, with a little time and patience, create a wall decoration at very little cost. A stencil is all that's needed and, if you stick to a design made of simple squares and circles, it is no problem to cut out a stencil for yourself. Alternatively, it is worth looking at the commercial stencils available. There are so many designs to choose from, you are certain to find one to suit your room.

YOU WILL NEED

- emulsion paint in blue, yellow and red
- paintbrushes
- scrap paper
- pencil
- ruler
- pair of compasses
- MDF
- tape measure
- saw
- acetate sheet
- craft knife
- self-healing cutting mat
- masking tape
- stencil brush
- small artist's brush
- rubber
- clear varnish
- varnish brush
- screw eyelets
- picture-hanging wire
- picture hook
- hammer
- drill, with masonry and wood bits (optional)
- rawl plugs (optional)
- wood screws (optional)

1 Choose your colours. You may consider complementing your existing furnishings.

2 Plan out the whole design to scale on paper. Here, a wrapping paper design was used for inspiration.

3 Cut the MDF to size and then apply the blue base coat.

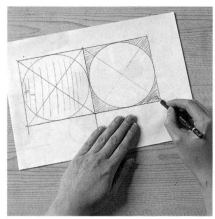

5 Use a ruler and compasses to draw the stencil on the sheet of acetate.

7 Tape the stencil over one of the squares on the grid. Stencil all the yellow circles and surrounds.

4 Draw a grid of squares on the painted MDF.

6 Cut out the stencil carefully using the craft knife on a cutting mat.

8 Stencil all the red circles and surrounds in the same way. ⟶

9 Touch up any smudges with the artist's brush.

10 Rub out any visible pencil lines.

11 Apply a coat of varnish. Attach the wall-board to the wall by inserting screw eyelets and stringing picture-hanging wire between them. Hammer in a strong picture hook and hang the board as you would a painting. Alternatively, drill holes in the wall and insert rawl plugs, screw the board to the wall and fill and make good the screw holes.

Right: Tailor the colours and shapes of a geometric design to pick up details of your existing interior scheme and produce the perfect wall decoration for your room.

STRETCHED FABRIC WALL

No special sewing skills are needed to achieve this dramatic wall treatment. Draping fabric on a wall is a good way to disguise lumps and bumps and add a lot of interest for little effort. When you have a modern fabric design, however, such as this eye-catching blanket, it may not seem appropriate to drape it on the wall in baroque folds. Instead, create a contemporary look by pulling it as taut as possible with coloured string at the corners and middle of the fabric.

YOU WILL NEED

♦ tape measure
♦ fabric or blanket
♦ pencil
♦ drill, with masonry bit
♦ rawl plugs
♦ screw eyelets
♦ coloured string
♦ matching strong cotton thread

1 Measure the fabric or blanket and mark the positions for the screw eyelets on the wall, bearing in mind that you want the fabric to be pulled taut. Drill and insert rawl plugs at the pencil marks.

2 Screw the eyelets into the wall.

3 Wrap lengths of string tightly around the corners of the fabric and around a small pinch of fabric in the middle of the two long edges.

4 Bind the string with cotton, leaving a long end. Feed the strings through the eyelets and secure them by looping the string back on itself. Finish neatly with the long ends of cotton.

ESCHER-STYLE WALL

Intricate "three-dimensional" designs, inspired by the trompe-l'œil drawings of the artist Escher, look stunning on a wall on which you want to make a real impact. Walls of any room of the house would take this idea well and it would be especially effective in a hallway. The description of how to construct the design sounds complicated but, in fact, once you have begun cutting out and assembling it, it soon becomes obvious how the shapes fit together. The beauty of Escher's designs is that all the components relate logically to one another in proportion and shape so that, once you have got going, the design practically assembles itself.

YOU WILL NEED

- ♦ scrap paper
- ♦ pencil
- ♦ metal ruler
- ♦ paper in light grey, dark grey and black
- ♦ craft knife
- ♦ self-healing cutting mat
- ♦ straight edge
- ♦ spirit level or plumb line
- ♦ wallpaper paste
- ♦ pasting brush
- ♦ clear varnish
- ♦ varnish brush

1 Plan and draw the whole pattern to scale on paper or refer to the diagram at the back of the book.

2 Decide on the colours of paper you want to use; choose three tones of the same colour to achieve a three-dimensional effect.

3 Measure the paper. Divide a sheet of the light grey paper into three.

4 Measure in from the edge to the depth of the large grey triangle shapes that form the border and mark the points of the triangles.

5 Draw the diagonals to make the triangle shapes.

6 Cut out the large light and dark grey triangle and diamond shapes, using the craft knife on a cutting mat. You will find that, once you have cut one shape, you will be able to use it as a template for others, because of the way the shapes relate to one another.

7 Draw the smaller light and dark grey diamonds which make two "sides" of the small "boxes".

8 Cut out the smaller diamonds.

9 Cut out the large and small black shapes.

10 Using a plumb line or spirit level and straight edge, draw vertical lines on the wall the same width as the large grey shapes.

11 Paste all the shapes into place with wallpaper paste and a brush. Smooth out any wrinkles with the palms of your hands. Give the design two coats of protective varnish.

Right: This type of design is so powerful in itself that it is at its best as a focal point. Leave everything around it as simple as possible; don't use it in a cluttered environment.

COLOURED STRING EMBROIDERY

The idea of decorating a wall with coloured string wound around tacks might evoke thoughts of nursery-school crafts; but it's surprising what wonderfully graphic patterns you can achieve. Set out a grid of tacks on the wall — substitute picture tacks if the wall won't take ordinary ones — and then you are set to create any design you want. Just wind the string around, either running the decoration across a wall from side to side or using it to make interesting borders.

YOU WILL NEED

♦ spirit level

♦ straight edge

♦ pencil

♦ tacks

♦ tack hammer

♦ emulsion paint to match existing wall colour

♦ paintbrush

♦ coloured string

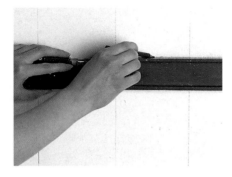

1 Draw a grid on the wall, using the spirit level and straight edge.

2 Knock in the tacks at all the cross points of the grid and all around the outside edges.

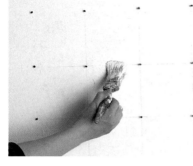

3 Paint out the pencil lines in the existing wall colour.

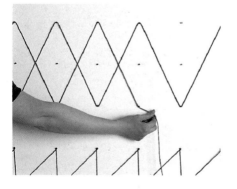

4 Arrange the string. Either buy coloured string or dip plain string in coloured paint to get exactly the colours you want. Wind the string tightly around the tacks, and start and finish with neat loops.

FILIGREE WOODEN PANEL

Radiator panelling need not only be used for its original purpose; it often comes in a variety of interesting designs that make it worth using over a much larger area. Turn it on its side and attach it above a skirting board, to bring it up to dado-rail height.

YOU WILL NEED

- ♦ scrap paper
- ♦ pencil
- ♦ ruler
- ♦ radiator panelling
- ♦ white chinagraph pencil
- ♦ jig-saw or hacksaw
- ♦ emulsion paint in 2 colours
- ♦ paintbrushes
- ♦ paint roller
- ♦ paint-mixing tray
- ♦ spirit level
- ♦ straight edge
- ♦ drill, with masonry and wood bits
- ♦ rawl plugs
- ♦ hammer
- ♦ wood screws
- ♦ glue gun and glue sticks

1 Plan and draw the overall pattern to scale on paper. Look at the panelling and decide what cuts will be necessary to make a border design.

2 Mark off the sections that will need to be cut with the chinagraph pencil.

3 Cut out the marked-off sections using a jig-saw or hacksaw.

4 Decide on your colours, bearing in mind that the background colour must be strong enough to show well through the panelling. You may need to mix colours to achieve exactly the shades you want.

5 Paint the wall and leave to dry. Meanwhile, paint the panelling.

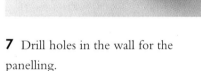

7 Drill holes in the wall for the panelling.

9 Drill holes in the panelling to correspond with the rawl plugs.

6 Using a spirit level and straight edge, mark a horizontal guideline for attaching the panelling.

8 Hammer rawl plugs into the holes.

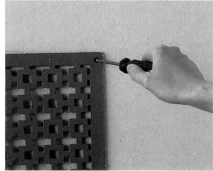

10 Screw the panelling in position on the wall.

11 Glue the panelling to the wall here and there, with the glue gun, to hold it flat against the wall. Then attach the border above. You can place a dado rail between the two.

Right: Radiator panels lend themselves perfectly to making unusual wall coverings.

COLOURED WOODEN BATTENS

Sometimes the simplest ideas are the most effective. Strips of wood at regular intervals can look most dramatic. Use them on one wall, or in smaller areas, such as the back of alcoves. The key is to keep the colours either toning or very contrasting and bold. If time permits, paint the top and bottom of the wood in different shades to add extra interest. The strips here are 5 x 2.5 cm/2 x 1in.

YOU WILL NEED

♦ tape measure

♦ wood strips

♦ pencil

♦ saw

♦ emulsion paint in 1 or more colours

♦ paintbrush

♦ spirit level

♦ drill, with masonry and wood bits

♦ rawl plugs

♦ wood screws

♦ ruler

1 Measure the height and width of the wall, to make sure you have equal spacing right up the wall. Cut the wood strips to the required length.

2 Paint the wood strips: you could paint all three sides that will show in different colours or tones, for a more interesting look.

3 Use a spirit level to mark a guideline for the first strip, to make sure the wood is absolutely level. Drill holes in the wall and insert rawl plugs. Drill holes in the wood and then screw the strip in place.

4 Mark out the position for the next wood strip; the space between strips needs to be absolutely even, to create the right effect.

PUNCHED TIN FOLK-ART WALL

Punched tin designs are surprisingly interesting and effective. They are a staple technique of folk-art interiors, but in this context they are often kept to quite small areas. However, there's no reason why punched tin can't be used over a much larger area, where it will look much more dramatic. You will need to frame the tin in some way, so it makes sense to put it above a dado rail; it could be bordered at the top by a picture rail. Another idea would be to enclose it within mouldings to form panels on the wall.

YOU WILL NEED

- ◆ scrap paper
- ◆ pencil
- ◆ thin tin sheet
- ◆ metal file
- ◆ long metal ruler
- ◆ chinagraph pencil
- ◆ metal punch
- ◆ tack hammer
- ◆ wood offcut
- ◆ drill, with metal and masonry bits
- ◆ spirit level
- ◆ straight edge
- ◆ rawl plugs
- ◆ dome-headed screws
- ◆ screwdriver
- ◆ clear varnish or lacquer
- ◆ varnish brush

1 Design and draw the pattern to scale on paper first.

2 Use a metal file to smooth any rough edges on the metal sheet.

3 Draw the pattern to size on the reverse side of the metal sheet using a chinagraph pencil.

4 Practise punching on a spare scrap of metal to get a feel for how hard you need to punch.

5 Punch out the pattern. Put a piece of wood behind the tin to protect your work surface.

6 Drill holes in the corners of the metal sheet.

7 Using a spirit level and straight edge, draw horizontal guidelines on the wall to indicate the position of the metal sheet. Drill holes in the wall where the corners will be. Insert rawl plugs in the holes.

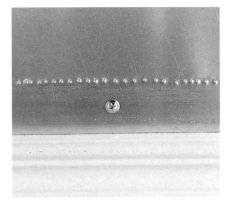

8 Screw the metal sheet in position on the wall.

9 Finish with a protective coat of varnish or lacquer.

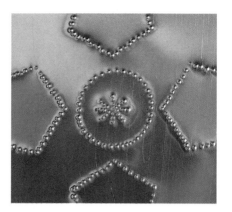

Above: The punched design is simple yet effective.

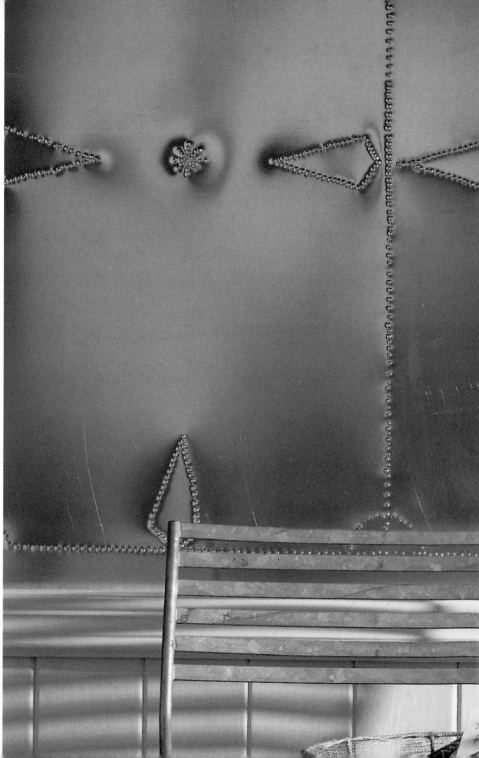

Right: However it is used, tin's reflective qualities make it an attractive option for a dull corner or gloomy hallway.

CURVING ROPE DESIGN

A pattern in rope makes a simple, textured wall finish, perfectly in keeping with today's trend for natural materials in interiors. As rope makes good curves, the design can be as twisting as you like. For a small area or to make a focal point in a room, mark out squares and put a different, simple design in each square.

You could also use the rope to create borders at dado-rail and picture-rail height.

YOU WILL NEED

♦ scrap paper

♦ pencil

♦ spirit level

♦ straight edge

♦ rope

♦ glue gun and glue sticks or strong adhesive

♦ masking tape

♦ craft knife

♦ white emulsion paint

♦ paintbrush

1 Plan and draw your design to scale on paper.

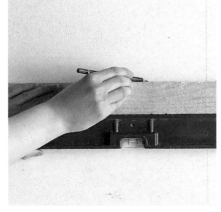

2 Transfer your design to the wall using a spirit level and straight edge.

3 Use a glue gun or other suitable adhesive to attach the rope to the wall. Use paint cans or other round objects to help you to make smooth curves. It is easier to cut the rope if you wrap masking tape around it, and cut through the tape.

4 Paint over the wall and rope with white emulsion paint; you may need a few coats to get an even finish.

PLASTER STARS

Plaster has a powdery quality and a pure white colour, which make it an especially interesting wall embellishment. Most decorative plaster firms have lots of simple shapes to choose from and will make a mould of anything you like, so the possible variations of this effect are endless. This idea works well as a border above a skirting board or around a door, as well as in a defined area, such as behind a wash basin.

YOU WILL NEED
- plaster stars
- scissors
- masking tape
- PVA glue or clear varnish
- paintbrush
- wall adhesive
- wood offcut

1 Decide on the design and spacing of the stars by making photocopies of them, cutting them out and using small pieces of masking tape to attach them to the wall. Try out a few versions until you're happy.

2 Seal the stars with a coat of PVA glue diluted with water, or with clear varnish. Leave to dry.

3 Follow the wall adhesive manufacturer's instructions for attaching the stars to the walls. Use a wood offcut as a spacer for positioning the stars on the wall.

MATERIALS

Wall dressing is all about looking beyond mere paint and wallpaper but you will, of course, find that conventional materials are necessary to get the job done. A good selection of brushes and rollers for applying paint are essential. Tacks, bulldog clips and screw eyelets can all be used for fixing, hanging and tying, while a tape measure or ruler, pencil or chalk and masking tape will help you mark out the area so your design appears on the wall exactly as you imagined it. Whether the look is controlled regularity, or more free-form, be sure to plan and mark out the design carefully before you begin, to avoid any nasty surprises. String and a plumb line will help you get the vertical lines right, and a spirit level will ensure the horizontals are exact. Decorating materials might include high-density foam, which can be cut or carved to the design you require to make a stamp for printing directly on to the wall. Keep your eyes open for materials to apply for decoration, from upholstery tacks to fabric wall hangings, filigree radiator panels to plaster shapes. Builders' merchants, yachting chandlers and haberdashers all stock interesting bits and pieces that serve a practical purpose, but can also be used to decorative effect.

Right: Wall dressing materials might include: bulldog clips (1); wallpaper roller (2); paste brush (3); patterned fabric (4); radiator panelling (5); chalk plumbline (6); upholstery tacks (7); screw eyelets (8); broken china for mosaics (9); tape measure and ruler (10); pencil (11); eraser (12); drill bit (13); metal punch (14); paintbrushes (15); plumbline (16); chalks (17); masking tape (18); craft knife (19).

TECHNIQUES

No matter what technique or method you use to embellish your wall areas, be sure to look at the condition of the surfaces before you start. The following tips may be useful if your walls are not in the best condition.

Filling defects in wood

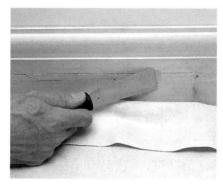

1 Fill splits and dents in wood using wood filler on painted surfaces, and tinted wood stopper on new or stripped woods that will be varnished.

2 Use your finger or the corner of a filling knife to work the filler into recesses and other awkard-to-reach places. Smooth off the excess filler before it dries.

3 When the filler or wood stopper has hardened completely, use sandpaper wrapped around a sanding block to sand the repair down flush.

Preparing painted woodwork

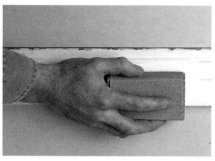

1 Use fine-grade sandpaper wrapped around a sanding block to remove any roughness, and to provide a key for the new paint to adhere to.

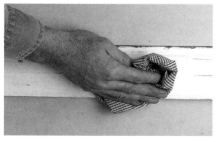

2 Wash the surface down with detergent or sugar soap to remove dirt, finger marks and grease, and to clean any dust left from sanding. Rinse with clean water, ensuring that no detergent residue is left.

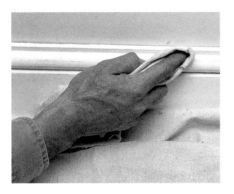

3 Use a clean cloth moistened with white spirit to remove dust from recessed mouldings and other awkward corners.

Filling cracks in plaster

1 Use the corner of a filling knife to rake out loose material along the line of the crack, and to undercut the edges slightly so that the filler has a better grip.

2 Brush out dust and debris from the crack, using an old paintbrush. Alternatively, use the crevice nozzle attachment of a vacuum cleaner.

3 Dampen the surrounding area with water from a garden spray gun to prevent it from drying out the filler too quickly and causing it to crack.

4 Mix up some filler on a board to a firm consistency.

5 Use a filling knife to press the filler well into the crack, drawing the blade across it, then along it. Leave the repair slightly proud of the surface When the filler has hardened, wrap fine-grade sandpaper around a sanding block and smooth the repair flush with the wall.

TEMPLATES

Flag Stencils

Mathematical Montage

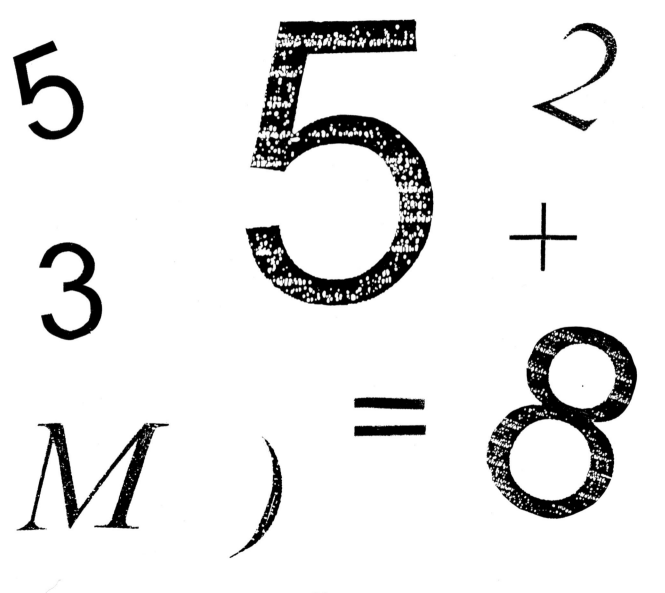

Escher-style Wall

SUPPLIERS

Most of the materials used in this book can be found in good hardwear suppliers: paints, brushes, wood and decorative mouldings are easily obtained. Some specialist shops are worth a visit. Consult your local yellow pages for yachting chandlers, specialty paper shops and haberdashers, among others.

Arthur Beale Ltd
Yachting Chandlers
194 Shafsbury Avenue
London WC2
(rope and jute)

C F Anderson and Son Ltd
Harris Wharf
Graham Street
London N1
(chipboards, hardboards, MDF, plywoods, timber and moulding)

Crown Paints
Crown Decorative Products Ltd
PO Box 37
Crown House
Hollins Road
Darwen, Lancashire

Paperchase
213 Tottenham Court Road
London W1
(decorative and textured papers)

Acknowledgements:
The author and publishers would like to thank Sarah Pullin and Kit Poulson for all their hard work in the studio.

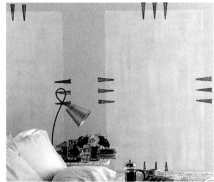

INDEX